EATING ACROSS AMERICA

A Foodie's Guide to Food Trucks, Street Food and the Best Dish in Each State

DAYMON "DAYM DROPS" PATTERSON

For permission requests, please contact the publisher at:

Mango Publishing Group
2850 Douglas Road, 3rd Floor
Coral Gables, FL 33134 U.S.A.
info@mango.bz

For special orders, quantity sales, course adoptions and corporate sales, please email the publisher at sales@mango.bz. For trade and wholesale sales, please contact Ingram Publisher Services at: customer.service@ingramcontent.com or +1.800.509.4887.

Daymon "Daym Drops" Patterson

Eating Across America: A Foodie's Guide to Food Trucks, Street Food and the Best Dish in Each State

ISBN: (paperback) 978-1-63353-686-9, (ebook) 978-1-63353-688-3
Library of Congress Control Number: 2017951054
BISAC—TRV031000 TRAVEL / Food, Lodging & Transportation / Road Travel

Printed in the United States of America

> *He went from Ashy to Classy*
> —Biggie Smalls from his *Sky's the Limit* Track

I am dedicating this book to my children, Daijah and Kaitlyn Patterson— those two girls changed my life indefinitely. I am not perfect but my girls give me THE CLOSEST FEELING TO PERFECTION for both of them!

PRAISE

" *Having become friends with Daym Drops–after he hilariously, and quite candidly, reviewed my family's Wahlburgers restaurant–I quickly realized that behind the outrageous comedy of his uniquely outrageous Internet food reviews, is an incredibly unique man. A man with a giant heart, matched only by his giant frame and equally giant appetite. But, whether you know him personally or not, one thing is clear to anyone who's laughed their asses off to his culinary critiques–Daym Drops knows food! As a food critic, and as a friend, I give him five stars–and you better believe the screen is shaking too, foodie fam!* "*
—Donnie Wahlberg, co-owner of Wahlburgers

" *A cool humble talented dude that stay working on the next move #truehustler.* "
—Regg Lester (Big Regg), CBS radio, WZMX Hartford

" *Met Daym a little bit before the song, "No New Friends" came out. Had I listened to them I would've missed out on having a Brotha' from another mother. Easily one of the most down to earth dudes on the planet. Glad to have him as somebody I consider family.* "
—Reginald Lewis

" *Daym is like the older, louder (not as good looking) version of myself (though he is from Stratford, we forgive him) "insider." He is the coolest Big Brotha' you could ask for.* "
—JT

66 *This man has a heart of gold. Always taking care of others, before himself and he is an amazing father! The world knows him as Daym Drops but I am fortunate enough to call him my Husband!* 99

—Ramyr Patterson

66 *Daym is doing the two things I love the most; eating and traveling but the difference between us is that he gets paid to do it.* 99

—Jaye Karl

66 *Working with Daym over the years has been a blessing and a great lesson. When you set your goals and put your feet into action, just about everything is possible. He never gave up on me and I do not plan to let him down anytime soon!* 99

—Edward Dupass

66 *It was a cold LA afternoon sometime around 2013. I was gearing up to bang out a YouTube collab video with some of the internet's most promising stars. In walks a man I only knew of as a legend. A man, larger than life not only in reputation, but in stature. For me, I had one job that day. Create a meal that would rival this man's past food reviews and make an impression on his taste bud brain. This man, was Daymon Patterson, aka Daym Drops. We hit it off right away and our friendship was birthed. If there's another person's taste buds that I would take into battle, it would be Daym's.* 99

—Josh Elkin, Host for Cooking Channel's *Sugar Showdown*

CONTENTS

PREFACE

Who knows? Perhaps I am looked at as the man about town who could truly appreciate his food experiences when the food brings MORE than just character to my palette.

White table cloth Michelin star dining rooms and hot dog vendors at Central Park all have one thing in common: experience. They all want you to not just taste the food, but to experience it.

I want the full experience when it comes down to each bite. There are times that I sit in my vehicle, just thinking *where should I go next for a food review?* I want to be inspired by my food. Inspired in a way that I can look directly into the camera and scream out upon the mountaintops just how GOOD this burger, chicken sandwich, pizza, taco, hot dog truly is; but in my line of work, that is not always the case.

I do not always get lost in the moment of pure tasteful bliss and more times than not, I am met with some foods that should have never made it to the menu. But because we spend our hard-earned money everywhere, from 5-star dishes to a fast food burger, our expectations tend to be that we should be met with value worthy of our time for each bite…but that's not always the case. THAT is where I come in: The YouTube Food Titan.

I hope that this guide helps you get closer to your taste buds. By the last page I want you to understand what food means; what the experience of eating from a food truck or cheap eats dive actually means to the cooks, the chefs, the owners, and most importantly, you. So let's get started!

INTRODUCTION

A CRASH COURSE ON FOOD TRUCKS AND CHEAP EATS

If you're familiar with my channel, you'll know that my dining experience tends to center on my car's dashboard. For a YouTube food review, it is the BEST option for enjoying and detailing what makes a certain order stand out. With that in mind, I was inspired to think of all the unique ways we enjoy food: family dinners, BBQs with friends, picnics, happy hour sliders, fish tacos and so many more. With all these different ways to eat and connect, I thought we'd start off with the community. And nothing brings people together quite like food made by hard-working, caring people. While you can find these dishes all across the restaurant world, I find that the ones that speak to me come from trucks and Mom and Pop spots.

Food trucks are a traveling person's best friend. Regardless if you are a block away from home or exploring the streets of Italy, you may not always be looking for a restaurant to sit down in. Sometimes you want to be by the water or roam about the city on your lunch break. Most areas will have a food truck posted nearby with some amazing hidden gems when it comes down to selection.

Have you ever been inside of a food truck? Do allow me to take you for a mental tour. On the passenger's side of the truck, we slide that door back and walk up two steps; all to be met at times with another door to our immediate left.

Venezuela + Italia

CONTEMPORARY GOURMET AREPAS

CAMINANTE

CAMINANTE

Once you slide this door back, you have just enough room for perhaps two or three people at best to work in what looks to be a small kitchen area, equipped with a grill(s), storage space, and their respective inventory to ensure they can get several hungry souls through their lunch breaks.

Now, I will not say that every food truck experience will be a good one. If those working the grill have no understanding of what it takes to prepare an amazing dish, your money and time will be quickly wasted. But let me tell you right now, should you have the patience to wait after you order that Lobster Roll, that Philly Style Cheesesteak, that free-range chicken sandwich, or a stuffed potato that could challenge a half loaf of bread in size, you will quickly be taken to foodie heaven. That initial bite and the burst of flavor alone will remind you that the wait was truly worth it!

The convenience of a food truck is that it moves about from place to place. If you can pinpoint a schedule by checking their websites and/or social media platforms, it is a short ride (depending on where you are) to take on something that may be new for you. Perhaps you never thought a food truck would be a great source to get something worthwhile, but let me tell you, most trucks that I have come across in my travels and at local events serve up the type of delightful selections that would challenge a few 4-star restaurants right now!

Never count out the underdog in the big game, for they too keep many tricks and treats up their sleeves that keep the locals and those abroad coming back for more. And customers tell their friends DAILY about their overall experiences.

The operational costs of a food truck are not cheap, and so to ensure they can continue to service the community, you will notice that not all foods prepared for you will ever challenge that of something found on a dollar menu. So, expect to pay a little more for what you crave, but more often than not, it is truly worth it.

Your pockets are light and payday is not necessarily around the corner, but your stomach has been talking to you all morning on your way to work. Let's explore a few cheap eats at local Mom & Pop spots. These venues can help curb your hunger with a price point that can and will satisfy you just as much as their menu.

It is no secret that you can find some amazing dishes at any Mom and Pop establishment. The local diners are filled with items that will have you sitting back with a smile, and the feel of being home amongst family is found at many of these locations.

Are you craving fluffy buttermilk pancakes, two eggs fried hard (lightly salted), and some hash browns with a coffee all for under $6.00? Well, if you are dining at one of these local locations, that is exactly what you will receive for that price point.

I simply love searching for restaurants that are clean once I step inside, mixed with a friendly atmosphere and a team that knows how to make you feel like you are part of their family. Again, to me that overall experience does more in terms of making me return and speaking highly of the place than a location that serves up quality food but lacks personality.

We all know great locations to visit, when it comes to food that sets your soul free for a low price. In today's society, where we are ripping and running around just to meet deadlines and make ends meet, that mental vacation to finally sit and enjoy a good meal becomes that little place of peace and relaxation that we all need at times.

When I think about it, we tend to feel as if we won the lotto when fed a meal to fit queens and kings. To then see a tab for it all with the total so low, your tip for great service can match the bill itself, should you be so generous.

Yet maybe you do not have an hour to spare and the next fifteen minutes need to be your fifteen minutes to pick up a quick bite and get right back to the hustle! So, you find yourself at the local QSR (Quick Service Restaurant), better known as fast food. By now this is nothing new to you; you have been here a million times before and unless they are offering something new on the menu, it is your go-to. It may be your #6, and unless they drop the ball in the kitchen, you know that the #6 will be your boost to get you through the rest of the day until dinner.

That double patty is seasoned to near perfection and topped with three partially broken strips of extra crispy bacon. The patties and bacon are gracefully complemented by some processed cheese that has an unbinding flavor of happiness, and there is something about that portion of grease that drips from the patties after your first bite that makes you recall your youth. Happier than a child in a candy store when your parents would pull into a McDonalds and get that Happy Meal for you, all so you can tear through the French fries, gobble down a few nuggets and land somewhere at the toy as you sip away at your orange drink.

These are the feelings that come rushing in as you sit in your car on your lunch break, perhaps dreading the very thought of going back to work. But, time waits for no one and bills must be paid! After scarfing down the delights of your fast food, which promises guaranteed satisfaction to a point, you are back on the job!

Now some people bring their own lunch to work, but when that time is not in your favor, the one thing that you can count on is the fact that at nearly every block or so, you will find a fast food location that is more than willing to assist your hunger. Each menu has been divided into specialty groups to choose from with a price point that is respectable for most QSR locations. At times, you can even catch a deal where you can receive a two-for-one special, that is when your eyes widen to match the smile upon your face. Who does not like two chicken sandwiches for the price of one at their favorite fast food establishment?

Fast food in general has been the resting home for the working woman and man for years. They have reached a large number of households, helping families get through another grueling and challenging workday. For the most part, you will always find something on the menu from salads to burgers that will fit the moment, and most importantly, fit your budget and get you over the hump.

AN ODE TO FOOD, FAMILY, FRIENDS AND HOME COOKING

When it comes to food, I am the all-around guy that has mastered the arts of determination, dedication and disasters! When I say disasters, let us just say that I am not one who should ever be in the kitchen telling someone HOW to cook, let alone cooking myself. It wasn't long ago when I tried my hand at making dough from scratch for some pepperoni bagel bites. I had everything necessary from the mixing bowl to the instant yeast to make my dough rise to the occasion.

Perhaps I did not mix the yeast in the water properly, but it looked close enough to the image that I had seen on YouTube and so I continued trying to make the dough. Things seemed to go smooth until it was time to remove the dough from the bowl and place it in my mixer, at which point my sticky bun dough did not settle the right way and I had the nastiest looking super dough balls that one could imagine.

After the time spent to remove all my sticky dough from the mixer and every single part that the dough had stuck to, I tried to ride that horse once again. The second time was a better attempt, but again, as with anything, practice makes perfect. I always like to say that food is the universal language, and over the years in my travels I have met and dined with a number of interesting minds.

My family is close knit and come Thanksgiving, you will find yourself surrounded by wisdom right on down to the young ones in the family. We will all be sharing what we are truly thankful for as the scent of the cinnamon escapes from the candied yams or the subtle calling of being down south graces the table with its presence within the greens, cornbread, ham, black eyed peas, baked macaroni and cheese and chicken.

You are in for quite a treat when the family is full of stories, but what is most important is the time spent and the time shared with those who you have not seen for a while. Have you noticed that good food is often part of the foundation within a good family? You can be at a family cookout and everyone knows to ask who made what. We all have our favorite foods prepared by various family members. So you look for that person at these functions and ask where their famous meal is located, for people simply love to be connected to good food at the end of the day.

What stands out about a home cooked meal is that you can actually taste the LOVE and preparation in these dishes. My Aunt Lisa is known for just about all of her dishes at our family gatherings, but I look for her Collard Greens. She makes them with a nice little kick, and when I speak of a kick I am talking about the spice level. Nothing too crazy, but among the pork fat saltiness broken down to a softer level for the chew and soaked within some tasty juices that help her collards maintain moisture, you are always in for a special treat with every bite.

My mother has held me down for YEARS when it comes to food from the heart. She is as hard a working woman as any. But, when I was young, after a long day on the job, my mother would come home tired as can be but still make time to stay up in a hot kitchen and whip up some of her BBQ Ribs. More times than not you would think they were smoked on a grill the way that meat would fall off the bone. It was often pointless to pick them up with your hands unless you wanted to sit there and suck on the bone. She did not stop there, her baked macaroni and cheese is what held it all together.

At first sight, you would see the crusted top of bread crumbs. The moment you cracked a spoon into that pan and took a scoop, you were pulling on cheese for days with steam exploding from each scoop as if a volcano was about to erupt!

Her sweet potato pie is always a sweet bite of delight. Remove that slice and catch the aroma of cinnamon and nutmeg about to dance around upon your taste buds, as the sweet and rich bite reminded you of everything right with life. She always used just the right amount of sugar so as not to make her sweet potato pie too sweet. There is no taking just one slice. Once you finish the piece in your hand, you run back in hopes something is left from a family that has just experienced the same sensational taste.

CHAPTER 1

WHO AM I?

THIS IS A QUESTION we may often ask ourselves going

through life. That journey to FIND who we are is a very important one; it dictates much of what our future holds. But first, we need to KNOW who we are to better understand our path.

I graduated from Platt Tech Regional Vocational Technical School in 1995. My goal to become a plumber was before me, it was my trade in high school and so my first day on the job fresh out of school was a complete FAIL. I recall working with my friend's father on a job, who was and still is a licensed plumber. He was ready to show me what it means to understand not only the customers, but also both residential and commercial plumbing.

My first job was to help remove an old cast iron piping system from a customer's basement. Cast Iron was decent many years ago and could be found in many homes abroad. But as the years passed, many quickly learned how cast iron would simply deteriorate and was expensive to repair due to how heavy the piping is and of course because cast iron is not cheap. Folks started moving over to plastic piping, which in my opinion is a world easier to work with, lighter and more cost effective.

I am following the plumber into a crawl space that is meant for short people, and just to catch you up to speed, fresh out of high school I stood at six foot four and weighed roughly 180 pounds. So here I am on my stomach, trying to worm my way through this crawl space and not bump my head every two seconds. As we are working at breaking away the cast iron I hear a crack and not long after the cast iron pipe drops rather close to my face. A few inches over and that would have been on my head. At that moment, I was sure this was probably NOT the life for me and so I started looking for an easier job.

Over the years I moved up the ladder in retail, for it seemed to be a great fit for me. I was able to talk to people all day and help them with their needs in Home Depot Plumbing (1996—2001) and working as an Assistant Manager for Lowe's Home Improvement (2005—2010). It wasn't until I started working as an Assistant Manager for Walmart that I decided to change from my regular posts on a website called YouTube, where I would post short skits and life vlogs, to reviewing food on my lunch breaks in 2009.

The reception on YouTube for these food reviews was more than I expected, with random people asking me to go to different fast food locations and review the latest and greatest thing on the menu. What attracts people to my channel is my honesty. If I do not like something, there is no changing, and I always say exactly what I feel with little regard to how any establishment feels about my thoughts. My reality is not what you see in a TV Commercial where everything is made to look amazing, and definitely not what you get once you arrive at the establishment. In my videos you get to see EXACTLY how the food is served up.

It wasn't until 2012 when I reviewed a double bacon cheeseburger at Five Guys that my life would change and go in a very different direction. Around this time, I noticed that more and more people were starting to do fast food reviews in their vehicles as well, though when I started out it was just me. I felt as if I was on to something great. Now, a community of food critics was being built. That Five Guys review drove my channel in a very different direction. It went viral with the help of a user "Zidar25" and a young man on my Facebook Friends list who contacted me and told me he put my Five Guys review on Reddit (a site that I knew nothing about back then and later found out is the front page of the Internet that will literally take you from the unknown to the known in a short matter of time). Reddit attention is what boosted my Five

Guys review from a few thousand views to literally a few hundred thousand within two days of receiving that Facebook message.

The news on YouTube caught wind of my rapidly growing video and the Gregory Brothers, known for Auto-Tune, reached out letting me know their thoughts and told me to check out how they turned my regular food review into a song called, "Oh My Dayum!" Instantly I fell in love with the song. From that moment, I entered my first major YouTube contract and they helped me shape my career on the platform, getting me linked with Maker Studios and events that I was part of.

The YouTube news of my video spread fast. Every news outlet jumped on the story and I started making a few TV appearances. In 2012, I signed a limited series contract with the Travel Channel for my own TV Show, *Best Daym Takeout* (which aired July 31, 2013). In the show I would travel to sample foods from three well known spots within each city, rate which of the three had the best bites, and award that location at the end of the show.

This attention placed me on episodes of Dr. Oz. Jimmy Fallon had me give him two exclusive food reviews that he did some amazing pieces on. That is how Rachael Ray found me, scooped me up quickly, and signed me to be the Food Correspondent on her show, which I have been for the past two seasons.

So, I tell people to put themselves out there when it comes to YouTube, you never know where this life will take you, but you have to be ready for what may come. There is no guide to success and fame, you will have to learn what works for you along the way. But YouTube has changed many lives over the years and made kids millionaires, when years ago you needed multiple degrees, wise investments, to be born into it, and/or hit the lotto just to see your first million. Kid stars are born every day with the way social media is set up.

So again, who am I? My name is Daymon Patterson, the "YouTube Food Titan" and welcome to *Eating Across America: A Foodie's Guide to Food Trucks, Street Food and Cheap Eats*.

CHAPTER 2

WHY YOUTUBE AND WHY FOOD REVIEWS?

MY STORY IS A UNIQUE ONE and I love to share it

when people ask, "What made you want to do food reviews?"

If you recall the old TV show on Travel Channel, *Man vs Food* with Adam Richman, he had (to me) the BEST JOB a person could have–eat food, travel and get paid for it! My only thought was, "How could I get that lucky?"

Now at this time, YouTube was still fairly new, but it was also a platform to film your passion as you saw fit. In mid-2009, I decided to start talking about the places that I would frequent on my lunch breaks at Walmart in Rocky Hill, Connecticut.

I mean, why not? I had a Kodak Playtouch (Vloggie Camera) that I would prop up on my steering wheel, look into the camera, and speak my mind on whatever I had for lunch that day from the surrounding fast food locations.

This all started out as nothing more than a hobby since I had an hour to kill on my break; and honestly, there was nothing else to do but sleep after I ate… until it was time to go back to work.

I started my YouTube adventure with a new food review each week and over time this started a small base of subscribers (that I would later start calling, Foodie Fam).

My Foodie Fam was made up of like-minded foodies who enjoyed my direct yet enthusiastic way of describing fast food. Over time they would start leaving comments as to where they wanted me to go next.

This interactive style of doing requested food reviews definitely helped to shape my YouTube channel. In all reality, the YouTube Community is who I strongly credit for my food review style and persona.

No fast food was considered SAFE! If I did not like something, biting my tongue at that moment was never an option. You are supposed to lay all of your cards on the table regardless of which QSR is being reviewed, good or bad. I gave the facts straight and broke down each bite with AUTHORITY!

Let us be honest with ourselves, when you watch a commercial all you will see are smiling faces that seem to be impressed by whatever the "next big thing" is at these fast food locations, and because it is a commercial, the food is made to look its best. But on the consumer end, certain locations fall FLAT on their delivery of what was shown in the commercial.

You get yourself ready for that first bite that then only sends your attitude quickly spiraling downhill into a pit of despair all over that new signature burger. What a great way to ruin your lunch, right?

This is how I would feel constantly on my lunch break. But no one knew... prior to my channel. But YouTube allows me a platform to verbalize those thoughts and share them with the masses. Ultimately, this created the brand, "Daym Drops."

Daym is part of my first name, Daymon, and Drops because (as I phrase it) I am dropping a new review each week. The channel name that you pick is important; it is the name that will represent you across all forms of social media and becomes a large footprint many others seek out over the years.

You want to choose something that best describes you and most definitely a name that speaks out LOUD AND CLEAR to the YouTube Community. This would be your next step after setting up your Google Ad Sense account as you begin learning the process and procedures of YouTube.

Perhaps you are thinking, "Why fast food?" When I look back on my YouTube Career, had I started with a healthier option not as easily accessible without travel versus doing a meal prep schedule at home, had I gone THAT route, would I be where I am today, working with Rachael Ray and executive chefs? Would THIS all still be my story? Perhaps it would be but in a very different way.

The In-Car Reviews would not be a "thing" on my YouTube channel. It was easy to determine that I should film more in-the-kitchen style videos and perhaps more sub channel videos along the way too.

However, I was always the traveling on-the-go type of man who would quickly choose the fast food options that are available on literally every corner, and so this is what brought me in the direction of wanting to talk about fast food on my YouTube channel. It always makes sense to speak your passion and what you know.

Oddly enough, as I began uploading videos of me sitting in the front seat of my vehicle, parked at the fast food spot for lunch on those days, the YouTube Community began watching more of my videos and sharing them with their friends and family. This is what helped me grow my audience. Keep in mind that growing your audience is only the beginning. When you are starting out it is easy to keep in touch with a percentage of those who are growing with you as a YouTube Creator, for you are receiving messages daily but not a heavy influx. So, taking the time to respond to almost everyone will not break you in a given day.

I highly suggest this communication for it truly helps your audience feel as if they are part of your growth. The difficult part is keeping up with everyone as your channel gets larger and you begin branching out on more social media platforms. The expectation for you to respond does not change and it will not be long before those who you literally spent months with in communication begin to feel forgotten as you do your best to keep up with all of the new messages flooding in. My recommendation is that you to find a sweet spot!

The POWER HOUR is where you will set aside time to respond to as many as you can; even if that is not everyone. At least you begin to open the dialogue and your base can send you messages. This interaction, where you are reminding them that they are truly appreciated and that without THEM you would not be where you are today, is what makes the videos worthwhile.

I work on that piece often, reminding myself that regardless of how busy I am…. I am this busy because of those who supported me up until this very point. So YES, when I see my Foodie Fam out and about, I will stop and take those pictures and/or sign those autographs because they supported me long before anyone else even knew about me. They are my foundation in this day-to-day hustle and the time spent with them, be it a few minutes or even an hour, means the world to me. You never know what a person is going through until you sit and talk with them, listen to their story, and offer up some kind words of advice along the way. Now, I am not perfect and more times than not I definitely drop the ball when it comes to just sitting down and responding. But I do make it a point to communicate with folks to see if I am falling too far away from the format they have come to enjoy on my channel–to determine if I should scale back and/or make changes.

The last thing that you want for your YouTube channel is for it to become stale, and so from time to time I spice it up by throwing visual curveballs into my Food Reviews–anything that changes the format that has pretty much been the same year after year. It is important to keep fresh and move forward with the times. The food review genre is a forever growing one. What worked for me several years ago is now the dinosaur of this age and I need to make the necessary changes to keep up with the demands of the people.

I look back on my old food reviews and for me it is important to see growth and strength in my personality. To excite myself from outside the box and know that I am delivering the very best in that review. Did I explain myself clearly? Did I showcase the product and give it a fair rating? What is missing and/or what do I need to change?

We should become our biggest critic and not just put videos out there without feeling as passionate about THIS VIDEO as we did our last. It does not take long for Creators to get in a rut and feel stuck or on autopilot putting out content to keep feeding the machine that is YouTube. Trying our best to keep up with analytics and find what companies want in order for ads to be placed against our videos is a way to lose who we are in order to make a dollar.

YouTube was a very different place years ago. We all uploaded content because we LOVED making it. Since we were not paid to do so, it was genuine content.

You would think that over the years not much would change, but once those checks started to roll in everything changed.... WE AS CREATORS CHANGED.

As with anything great, the greed for fame and money overpowered the art that was once YouTube. Many lost their way chasing the darkest place known to mankind. Now do not get me wrong, there is nothing bad about paying your bills. But once it gets to the point of stepping on another in order to make that happen, we have lost our way. That is where many YouTube Creators are today.

I will forever look at YouTube as my passion, for I simply enjoy putting out my body of work. The financial aspect is nice but there is so much more this platform has to offer, and once you stop chasing the darkness and see what amazing connections can be made, only then will that become the moment of greatness.

Food Reviews take on their own style after a while. Anyone can present food as they see fit and make it their own, but it is how you present it. Do you see the food as just food, or is it a part of you that can be made into a story?

Can you build a climactic moment and draw in an audience as you take them for a tour through the good, bad and the ugly of each bite?

I feel that we all have a food critic within and that unique character is dying to come out. But, we also bring out the very best of that critic within on a daily basis when we speak about our dining experiences.

We all know what we enjoy and we cannot tolerate. New experiences come our way when we take a chance and step out to try something that is new to our palette, and then we talk about it.

People have been doing food reviews for years, and what I do on YouTube is nothing different than what we all do when we are out and about.

I simply place a character to my madness and let the thoughts collide before a camera. But what about stepping out from my fast food shell and taking on the other side of this Foodie Life known as the Food Carts. Join me on the next leg of this adventure.

CHAPTER 3

FOOD CARTS

iKorean ❤ Twist

Korean ❤

Korean ❤

Korean Twist

MENU

Tacos
bite corn tortilla filled with your
favorite choice of protein, topped with
lettuce, carrots, bean sprout, cilantro
and home made sweet and spicy
BBQ sauce, and with our
creamy mayo dressing

•Single Taco	
•3 Tacos	$2.50
•Taco Combo	$6
(3 Tacos+Fried Rice+Kimchi Or Salad)	$7

Burrito
Large flour tortilla filled with your
favorite choice of protein broiled with
rice, lettuce, carrots, bean sprout,
cilantro, cabbage, and home made
sweet and spicy bbq sauce alongside our
creamy mayo dressing

•Burrito	$6.50
•Burrito Bowl	$6.50
(3 Corn Tortilla)	$7.50

Yakisoba
Japanese style noodles with vegetables
and your choice of

FOOD CARTS are found at just about every fair, carnival, sporting event, and concert. They make their homes near subway stations and financial districts. They feed the city. These are the street vendors that spend the better part of their morning preparing a few edible basics that will complement your food orders.

I find myself drawn to food carts for the unexpected. You never know what hidden gems you will find nestled between a traveling fire. If I want a flavor packed taco fish salad or a meat filled sloppy Joe, it is safe to say that my local food cart will be able to fill my order and keep me coming back for more. Keep in mind, these are mobile Mom & Pop carts and so the food quality overall is passionately different, for your food will be handled with more attention and care. These cart owners NEED your business and so they will go above and beyond to ensure the satisfaction of the customer.

Perhaps a group of friends simply knows of a food cart that reminds them of home. But how does anyone arrive at these carts in the first place? Part of the unexpected is the gambling aspect of the meal, the risk versus reward that heightens your taste buds. The best approach is trial and error. When venturing into any culinary adventure, it is crucial to understand the menu, the people, and the love. These are the carts that you truly want to embrace. If flavored the right way, every bite will put your soul at ease, knowing they took the time to cook up some of your delights the way your momma used to cook. This gives you all the reason to put your trust in food carts.

HOT SAUSAGES
100%BEEF
HALAL FOOD
HOT DOGS
HALAL FOOD
DELICIOUC
LAMB OVER RICE
GYRO
SHISH KEBAB
HOT SAUSAGE
FALAFEL
HOT DOG
on stick
PRETZEL DOG
HALAL FOOD
CHEESEBURGER
LAMB GYRO
HOT DOG
ITALIAN SAUSAGE
CHEESEBURGER
SHISH KEBAB
HOT KNISHES
Italian Sausage

It is no secret that I love to hunt down an amazing double bacon cheeseburger, but what I have come to learn over the years is that I find more of those burgers at food trucks versus food carts, and to be honest, I would love to come across a food cart that would serve up the type of burger fit for a KING! A burger that drops the right amount of grease, not enough to fill a shot glass, but just enough to lubricate the beef so that it is not overly dry. A burger that has cheese melted in whole, with flavor to enhance the experience. A burger with a slight touch of mayo, perhaps with toasted buns. And for the grand finale, extra crispy bacon layered, so that every bite is filled with delight.

Food carts are often filled with specialty items that make the cart distinct. What is amazing about these carts is the mobility and knowing that most folks within that general area will have access to these bites at any given time, should they follow the schedule of a food cart.

New York for me is a wonderful starting place if you are looking for a variety of carts. Street vendors are at the call of people around-the-clock. When you awake in the morning ready to face another day in Midtown, simply look out of your window and down at the food carts making their way to the corners where traffic often stands still, as do passersby waiting for the light to change.

Food carts are convenient and definitely help ease those hunger pains should you need a bite to hold you over until lunch and/or during lunch. Halal Guys are one of the better-known food carts in the city and rightfully so!

I recently had a chicken & beef gyro combo complete with falafels and a spicy sauce, that if not careful, will most definitely wake your taste buds and make you sweat! What helps take that spicy edge off is the rice, but the rice will not serve as a cure-all if you overdo it with the sauce, like I did.

You can taste the love in each bite, for the seasoning is blended within the meal. The tender bite of the meats and the simple fact that you get PLENTY to hold you over, with a price point that is actually respectable, makes you appreciate it that much more. However, the flavors of my combo are what make me want to come back to Halal Guys. If you have not experienced this middle eastern delight, you are missing out on the main source of what makes food amazing...PASSION!

Halal Guys is not alone when it comes to some amazing food carts in New York. You need to venture out and even get lost at times in the city to find some hidden gems. Regardless of your craving–a foot-long hot dog, deli sandwich, a burger, or even breakfast–there is a cart with your name on it and an experience to remember.

Creating the memories is half the fun; what is most important is with whom you choose to create these food mementoes. Getting the opinion of friends and/or family while you sample some delectable food cart specials is where you get the full understanding of what is good, great, or just terrible in the eyes of others, even if you personally cannot wait to take another bite.

Food has a voice and that voice has a range around the globe. I love to say that food is the universal language and that is simply because, regardless our choice, food is known to bring people together. In a society driven by people burying their faces into a cellphone and/or tablet, that breath of fresh air is a simple bite away.

So, the next time you are in the city and you happen to walk or drive near a food cart, I want you to stop and give it a try. Experience something outside your norm, you just might like it. Trust me, I am not the only crazy person who loves to talk food while standing around a food cart. Each vendor has their own great personality, influenced by how often they travel throughout the city. A simple conversation will have the next twenty minutes of your life open to new thoughts and ideas as to what you can do in the city while you are visiting.

While you are talking to that vendor, do not be afraid to ask which other local vendors serve up some good bites in the city. If you find yourself in the city for a few days, you just might want to stop by other food carts to see what they have to offer. Each cart has its own specials and a variety of options to choose from, but it all comes down to the foodie adventurer in you!

Do you have what it takes to eat your way through New York and or any other city that specializes in food carts? Do you mind venturing off and exploring an area on your own just to find some of these hidden gems and sharing the details with the masses?

We get comfortable in our day-to-day lives and it does not take long before we are fixed in on what we plan to do for lunch and dinner, but living outside the circle is where adventure truly begins. The opportunity to take a chance on who we are as individuals, to explore the world for something interesting and new, is often right outside our front door. Fear holds us back from doing more!

Well, now I am asking you to LIVE IN YOUR MOMENT and step outside to explore. Look for these food carts that I speak of and then take it a step farther…. Why not start up with some food trucks too?

Now you are probably thinking that I am CRAZY when I throw these trucks into the mix but why am I crazy?

Ok sure, carts and trucks are probably not the first thing that comes to mind when you ask, "What's for dinner?" but just think…. Why not take a chance on something different and more so if you've never had it before? Let's dive deeper into what the food truck game is all about, shall we?

FRENCH FRIES

FALAFEL SANDDWICH

urger   Philly Cheese Steak

ikifon Pita   Chicken over Rice

Cold Drinks
Water
Gatorade
Snapple

SLUSH

WATERMELON   GRAPE
ORANGE   CHERRY

Mister Soft

AKES

CHAPTER 4

FOOD TRUCKS

WHAT is there NOT to love about food trucks? I mean just think about it for a moment—you want something authentic but you do not have time to travel to your favorite restaurant for lunch. Suddenly, you recall that just up the block is a food truck that serves up some of the best Mexican dishes that you've ever had the pleasure to taste.

Now, keep this in mind and hold on while I take you through some of my food truck experiences, and of course why I appreciate the ease of access to these trucks.

In Chapter 3 we discussed food carts, and though they are not as easily accessible, once you are in the right area, BOOM! The magic begins to happen. But with food trucks, all you truly need to know is where everyone will be at lunchtime. Somewhere parked up near the water or around the town square will be a few trucks that can serve a few hundred hungry patrons or more.

"How may we serve you today?" I know that I am not the only person who loves to hear those words from any establishment, but when it is a hot day and the inside of that truck is quite possibly a few degrees beyond disrespectful, to still be greeted with such admiration is a beautiful thing.

You look back after reading the menu and begin with your order. The best part about it all is that your stomach is probably speaking to you in a world full of unknown languages. Yet, it is screaming out FOOD loud and clear, and so you begin to place your order.

Do note that you will have a little wait, but more often than not, that wait is so worth it! There is a reason that you return. You have been to this food truck a million times before and each return is like the first time you fell in love—this cannot be denied.

I come back to see what new menu items have been thought up since I was last there. What can I try next from this truck that will shock me? What does the next truck have that this one does not? Will my taste buds be blown away? Will it be a dish that needs a full-blown YouTube food review?

Options, my friends. Food trucks provide options, and that is what we crave! Be it a taco salad or the best grilled chicken you've had the pleasure to devour, food trucks can soothe the savage beast.

I am looking for presentation, honesty of the plate, taste, shock value—I want the full-on experience, as if I am walking into an amusement park for the first time not knowing what to expect. The moment I am on that ride, I am taken on a journey beyond compare! THAT is what I want from my food truck experience.

Will that Lobster Roll be filled with lobster that tastes as fresh as if caught that morning and prepared JUST FOR YOU? Will the butter be salted just enough, so when that first juicy bite hits your palette, you are taken aback by the flavor, thinking to yourself, "Could this really be LIFE right now, because this LOBSTER ROLL is giving me life in every single bite!"

Your time with any given food truck should be fun. Food is fun and we need to appreciate those who are spending endless hours creating something for people to enjoy.

Food is meant to be enjoyed or at least that is how I feel when I step out. I need to know that my hard-earned dollar is going towards something that I could not have easily been prepared at home. So yes, I want the full-on experience and I would like to try new creations that are out there. An amazing Chef can whip up just about anything, even some off-menu items, construct an abundance of food from a minimal list of ingredients, and make the plate work for a multitude of people at the drop of a dime.

When you hit your local food truck, that is what you are in search of. How creative your server will be, and though we respect them even more for the summer days working up a sweat inside of that truck, when they hand us our orders, we should easily be able to tell that we made the right choice by coming to one of our favorite spots.

So why a food truck and not a sit-down restaurant? That is truly your call, but just know that these food trucks are unique and drive out of their way at times simply to serve YOU! Restaurants are not going anywhere, unless they serve up bad food. Then expect them to close. We already know that at any given time we can drive out to some of our favorite restaurants and order what we are accustomed to from the menu. To me, food trucks are more at a personal level of service and can be found in the parking area of our places of employment or even down the street.

As you read these words I am sure that you can think of quite a few food trucks in your own area that deserve some recognition. Either the trucks that you frequent from time to time or perhaps the new trucks that you've seen in passing and finally decided to see what they have to offer. Whatever the case may be, food trucks have quickly expanded over the years; we need access to great bites regardless of our location.

I still get excited about food truck festivals, for that is the time that you can get together with your friends and find yourself surrounded by a plethora of trucks that are all offering up something different. Your entire day is spent hopping from truck to truck getting your fill of the foods that you've come to love.

If your first food truck experience is coming up be sure to write about it. Tell others exactly how you feel about the food, the servers, and presentation because, ultimately, we need more trucks on the streets. The fact that we need to drive out of our way before we find any trucks at all is terrible.

Let's work together to ensure growth! Again, we know that some of the BEST foods are found in a Mom & Pop location. Well that is exactly what you have here, but on wheels. The only way to ensure that we see more food trucks out and about is to support the current ones that are within our reach. So be sure to stop by your local food trucks and show that love. Step out from what you are accustomed to and try something new.

CHAPTER 5

CHEAP EATS

LET'S GET REAL, after paying bills and ensuring the basics are taken care of, we do what we need to do in order to make our cash stretch until the next pay day. Yet, with our busy schedules and the unpredictability of life, we may find those days or nights when we need to grab a bite and not break the bank while doing so.

Some of you know the best spots to eat at that still serve up some amazing food for the lowest price possible. You crave something more than a fast food chain, and your stomach is telling you that a baked chicken or garden salad is calling at this hour. And what hour is that? I used to call it the graveyard shift for those of us who worked the thankless hours overnight and were given a half hour to run out and make the 2:00 a.m. magic happen at whatever spot was open.

Once you grew tired of that run-out life and wanted to enjoy something that you had already prepared, it was simple enough. You made a quick run earlier in the week to your local grocery store to pick up some items that you could whip up for a nice weekly meal. Grocery shopping can become quite the challenge when your funds are low, and so you should quickly learn the fun behind coupons and double discounts. Trust me when I say that there are many people who have already figured this life out and would be more than willing to help teach you about it.

Once you hit the savings and find yourself spending only $30.00 for a grocery run that should have totaled $145.00, you fully understand what cheap eats are all about. Taking the moment to get yourself through another grueling week at the lowest cost possible!

RESTAURANT
WAVERLY
DINER
BREAKFAST
LUNCH
DINNER
BREAKFAST
LUNCH
DINNER
RESTAURANT
OPEN 7 DAYS
24 HOURS
ATM
WiFi
West 4 St Station
A C E B D F M
Elevator at W3 St & 6 Av

Still, the search for cheap eats continues from state to state, and if you ask a few locals during your visit, they will be able to point you in the right direction to have some amazing food that will not break your wallet in the process.

This is why supporting Mom & Pop locations is vital. More often than not, we can eat like champions at local spots and keep the tab under $10.00! Their prices tend to be so low, you find yourself leaving a generous tip.

I often find myself looking for these establishments, regardless of where I am. I want to know that we still value affordable quality in fresh foods. But quality is not as easily accessible for all, and so be sure to use food and restaurant apps that let you know where to go when you need something right now and you are also down to your last $25.00.

Another way to curb the cost is to look for the specials. I have a few restaurants around my way that love to whip up two bacon, egg and cheese sandwiches for breakfast for $3.00. In New Britain, Connecticut, I always find myself at Sahadi's Hotties and Willie Pep's. I frequent both locations often. They do not skimp on the food and neither location will charge you an arm and a leg just to eat. You will find LOVE being placed into each bite, and they are both great locations with an at-home feeling.

Willie Pep's is a family owned business that was built in honor of the late Willie Pep, a professional boxer from Connecticut who held the World Featherweight Championship in both 1947 and 1950.

When you walk in, you feel like you stepped into the past, with pictures of Willie on the walls and many of the great celebrities of his time. Each menu option is specially named with boxing references, and each bite will knock you out if you are not prepared!

What is better than to walk into an establishment with comfort food at low prices and owners who can share a wealth of knowledge from the past and greet every customer as if they are family? Honestly, this is the treatment that makes a Mom & Pop location simply AMAZING. But do not take my word for it—if you are ever in the Connecticut area, stop by Willie Pep's and tell them Daym Drops sent ya!

The truth of the matter is, whatever your desires may be, there should be a pit stop for you; a quick spot off the highway in your travels. I know what you are thinking, "Daym, I am NOT about to eat at some hanky looking diner off the highway that looks as if it sat in a ghost town for the last twenty years."

I know how you feel, but I would not discredit those locations just yet. We are talking about some respectable service and the search for good food at a low cost, correct? Why not give the unknown a try?

Many of us are accustomed to going to the locations that everyone is talking about. But think about it—before social media was our "how to" guide through life, it was the word on the street that brought many of us out. Walking by people hearing them say, "Did you try the home fries at…" prompted us to go to see just how good those home fries were! Well guess what? That hanky looking location IS the spot that I am telling you about, and maybe we need to go inside to see if they still got it!

Don't be so quick to pass judgement before you have the chance to sit inside a piece of history and live the moment.

Always share your finds with friends and family because we are all looking for a few spots where we can eat good food, and save money while doing so. However, don't simply tell your friends and family. Be sure to write about your experiences, and if you are not the type of person who enjoys writing, take some pictures and share your Foodie journey with those who follow you on social media.

We need more hidden gems exposed! We need more Mom & Pops brought to the forefront and talked about. And, most importantly, we need HISTORY to live on in this food game!

I love seeing older car hops brought back to life from the '70s and given a chance to feed a new generation.

There is a spot from my own past called "Crickets" that is currently being brought back. I remember, at the innocent age of seven, how we would all run to Crickets with whatever allowance money we had and get our favorite foods!

You could not beat their hotdogs, fried chicken wings, burgers and fries! They would whip up some of the thickest milkshakes in town. They were rich and creamy in taste. You needed a spoon to scoop them up because a straw just wouldn't cut it, and every flavor meant your taste buds were on their best behavior and were about to receive a treat that would make them smile with joy!

Crickets was the spot where everyone applied for a job the moment they were of age, but only a select few could say they had the honor of working there. The best part was that, with only a few dollars in your pocket, you knew that a five-dollar meal at Crickets meant you would be eating well, and the quality of the food could not be denied!

Even while writing this chapter, they are about to have the re-grand opening of Crickets in Stratford, Connecticut where I was born and raised. I already reached out to them and yes, over twenty-five years later, I will do a food review of the very car hop that I grew up with.

The only question is, will I still receive quality food at a low price? Only time will tell.

CHAPTER 6

HOLE IN THE WALL RESTAURANTS

WHAT IS THAT SMELL and why is it coming from this dark

alley? Well, that scent is love. That scent is what piques your interest. That scent is the first step. It's enough to make you venture out from your comfort zone and try something from a location that many would not normally frequent.

For a moment, I want to suspend reality and blindfold you. But this being a book, my editor suggests that we should probably not blindfold you. For this chapter we are going to remove both doubt and fear from you by questioning everything you thought you knew about food. Now let us go down this alley and follow the scent. Picture it as it leads us to a mangled screen door with no signs screaming the name of this establishment. But, from within, the essence of what we caught a mere whiff of on the streets, is now strong and we are sure that we have reached the location.

We can see light peeking through the windows and shadows of movement, so we open the mangled screen and turn the knob on the door slowly. The lights brighten as we walk in, and at first sight, we look at the years of flavor that have accumulated on the walls.

Like all hidden gems, it gives off the allusion of a ghost town with a few regulars hidden in the shadows. Two men sit at the booth on the right in a far corner, one with a newspaper in his hand and the other sipping on his coffee. Yet both are engaged in a conversation with each other as if it had been years since they last spoke.

Place mats are on the tables, with silverware and picnic cloth draped over the edges. This retro vibe has taken us back for a moment and as we look around embracing the ambiance of what is yet to come. You can tell that this place needed a touch of love, art, and a polished investor to come through and revamp the walls, but that can't silence the flavors. Like all mouth-watering spots across the nation, it's about the team putting in work on the stove in the kitchen. They are the ones that get you inside.

Finally, we are greeted and taken to our table. Instantly, we notice that our chairs must come with a weight capacity of 115 pounds, for the one leg that is shaking is probably screaming for mercy as my big bones settle in.

We notice that the placemat hosts a sticky residue as we try to move it from the tablecloth, but age and hard work live here, so do we run away or stay to see what they serve up? I say we stay, and so you open your menu that has the pages sticking together as well, and come across some of what I like to call, fan favorites!

This is what *Eating Across America* is truly all about! Regardless of the state we live in, we all have our restaurant fan favorites. But, I promise you not every location will be as spacious and visually entertaining as some of the hole in the wall establishments that also serve up a higher quality of food.

They say, "Never judge a book by its cover," so we need to treat these spots the same. Simply because they may not be in the greatest of areas does not mean that you will receive poor service and find a lack of something amazing to eat and enjoy with friends. Experience a better moment that involves removing yourself from your comfort zone and stepping out on a chance to be blown away by the quality of food that you are about to receive. One of the best meals you can enjoy in all of Baltimore, MD is in this tiny hole in the wall shack where they care only about the food. No frills or thrills or even plates – the food is actually served on a wooden table lined with newspaper. And yet there is nothing that compares to the taste, the ambiance and the experience.

Experience the moment made for the masses, to come together and discuss what makes food awesome. I want to ask, "Who is the Chef?" Because when the food is just that good, you'd like to put a face to the plate. And the best surprise of the day is when the tab arrives. You flip it open, and for all that you had to eat, the price is much lower than expected. So you leave something extra in the tip to both compliment the food and the service from a spot that most would pass by and not even give a second thought to.

Investments need to be made for upkeep and not every location will have financial backing for whatever reason, but we the people have a voice in this food game! We the people can speak up for these "not so visually sound" establishments simply by frequenting them and telling others to do the same.

Spread the word and fill the seats to the point where we help to make a difference and perhaps give the powers that be a reason to invest. There is no possible way change can exist without strength in numbers.

This might sound crazy but I want to blindfold you for just a second and tell you that where we are going is a surprise. I walk you to my vehicle and put you in the passenger side right before we take off to the destination.

Now I remove you from the vehicle and walk you up a few steps before you ask, "Do I smell cinnamon and coffee?" This much I confirm before telling you to watch your step and walk up four steps as I count each one. Then I open a door and walk you in.

That scent of coffee gets stronger and you ask me, "Oh great, I was hungry! How did you know?" You hear a woman ask about the blindfold and I tell her that this is a surprise for my friend before she seats us.

You ask to remove the "blindfold" but I tell you, "not until you've had a few bites of the food," and then I place our order. Shortly thereafter our food arrives and I tell you not to worry, for I will both butter and cut up your French toast. I hand you the fork with a decent bite of French toast on it and just a little syrup, then I sit back and wait….

Hesitant, you slowly bring the fork up to your mouth, but then you risk it all on that bite and your face hits a glow! After chewing, you taste the softness of the French toast and hint of cinnamon.

The sweetness from the maple syrup sings to your soul and you follow up with, "Ok, this is good!"

Now you instantly remove your blindfold and begin to look around and notice that this place would not have been your first choice, but you cannot deny the fact that they serve up some good dishes, as you look back down at your plate and continue with your meal.

When the experiment becomes an experience, that is when we speak highly about it, regardless of how it may look! Let us be honest, we KNOW good food when we taste it, and after a while, it no longer becomes much about where, but WHEN! When will we go back and try something else on their menu?

So now ask yourselves, WHEN was the last time you stepped away from the known and wandered off into the unknown to try something different? If it has been a while since you last sought out a hole in the wall to eat at, why not NOW? Why not TODAY? You may have to travel a bit farther than usual to find one but I am sure that one exists near where you live.

I want you to give that spot a chance, even if you are passing by on your travels. Take a chance on something different and do not be quick to judge what they may have to offer based solely on how the restaurant looks and/or its location.

You may walk out of there with a very different appreciation for these hole in the wall establishments and even a story to share with friends, for word of mouth goes farther than some can imagine. Be sure to jump on those review apps and leave your overall experience, let us build together and write these spots back into the limelight! If there is a second or third chance to be given, this would be that time, and we all truly make the difference as a united voice of forgotten restaurants. Understanding the dedication that is put forth to hopefully remain the choice of the people for years to come, but that is not always the case.

These establishments are filed at the bottom of the list and forgotten more times than not, and we lose a bit of history simply because it may not be as visually appealing in comparison to its competition up the street.

What is interesting is the fact that the competition, though new with all of the latest technology installed to keep any family entertained, falls short on some of its dishes. The flavors are subpar, creativity and the presentation are often in question, and you do not find yourself there as often.

These establishments do not last long for a reason and it is simply because they lost their way. Personally, I will choose a hole in the wall over most other choices, ANY DAY!

CHAPTER 7

TASTE BUDS

I WOULD LIKE TO THANK YOU for taking the time

to sit back, relax and read from my tales. Hopefully at least one chapter (if not a few) was able to help you see things a bit different in this food space and perhaps even nudge you in the right direction when it comes to making a last-minute decision to be part of something different. I may not be the type of man who likes to get in the kitchen and cook an amazing meal but I sure love to travel and talk about some of the amazing meals I have had. Now, let me tell you about a few of my friends who I like to eat with.

Now, when it comes to food, I will travel where necessary to get my hungry on. But my love for a great bite started with my own mother's cooking. This woman would work all day, get home in time to both check my homework, and of course cook up a new dish for me each night. Now I will admit, I was never one for leftovers and so my mother would literally cook something new each night. Of course, there were those occasions when I had no other choice but to eat leftovers, but they were far and few between.

My favorite dish growing up was basic–hot dogs, beans and bacon. You are probably looking at that a bit differently, but it is the truth. My father would pick me up on weekends for his time with me, even though he was dating a woman at the time. Instantaneously, I fell in love with hot dogs, beans and bacon, and when I was back with my mother that would be my go-to requested meal. I grew up a Jehovah's Witness and so my weeks determined the meals:

Monday—(Pasta) We did not have service on Mondays and so there was a bit more time to sit, talk and watch TV while my mother would whip up various pasta dishes.

Tuesday—(Hot Dogs Beans & Bacon) Something quick for we had service from 7:00—9:00 p.m. and so she had enough time to get home from work, whip that up for me and then iron our clothes for the Kingdom Hall that night.

Wednesday—(Pork Chops and Wild Rice) Now Mom would hook up some MEAN pork chops, seasoned just right. They had a bit of a tougher bite to them, but the way she would season those chops made my mouth water just thinking about them.

Thursday—(Mock Spaghetti) Being that we had Bite Study on this night from 7:00—8:00 p.m., she had enough time to hook up a faster version of spaghetti with some ground beef mixed in. But all the same, I would hook it up with a bit of sugar and Kool-Aid on the side to wash it down, and I was a happy camper.

Friday—(Take Out) After a week of cooking, my mother would want to ease into the well-deserved weekend, and so at times she would order some pizza. If not we would have Chinese food from the Hood Spot up the block. It all worked out and I still ate like a champion.

Saturday—(Ribs & Sides) When I tell you, "slide off the bone ribs" that is about ALL Mom would ever hook up! I would want ribs and deviled eggs! I know it does not sound like a great combination, but when you are young everything works in your favor! Corn on the cob would complement this dish and some rice for extra love.

Sunday—(Soul Food Sundays) This is what we all would look forward to in any household coming up. Collard greens, mashed potatoes, fried chicken, cornbread, candied yams, baked macaroni and cheese, and when the Holidays would call for it, "Hood Egg Nog!" but let's not get me started, I may never finish this chapter if we go too deep!

Dining with my mother was the beginning of my story, but dining with friends is where my adventure really begins.

Let us take my first food love, Hostess Honey Buns, introduced to me by my cousin Claude.

Growing up in Stratford, Connecticut we had a family owned store nearby called Turbo's News and this is where we would acquire all our penny candies. But when you had some allowance in your pocket from the week, it only made sense to upgrade those penny candies to bags of chips and hostess cakes.

On one special trip made to Turbos, Claude introduced me to the sweet and savory taste of a frosted Honey Bun that I would never forget.

Honey Buns are the childhood treat that elevated my taste buds and really introduced me to the sweet side of this Food Life.

With hungry friends like my boy Anthony, we would frequent some fun restaurants throughout Connecticut on a weekly basis. He is the complete opposite of me; standing at roughly five foot six and weighing in at 145 pounds soaking wet, his appetite would impress a number of professional food competitors.

On many occasions, I would think that Anthony had a tape worm that finished his food and kept him hungry, for he could eat me and three more versions of me under the table and wonder where his dessert was when he was done. Now THAT is what you call a Food Savage.

Being that we are both heavy gamers and have been for years, I can recall many days where ordering something simple as a pizza and wings would satisfy the hungry savages within. We would rip through a large sausage and pepperoni pizza while dipping our buffalo wings in some creamy ranch sauce as if it would be our final meal.

Both of us could easily be found at the likes of T.G.I. Fridays taking down a Jack Daniels Burger or at Sammy's in City Island having some succulent seafood bites. Anthony and I never had a problem traveling to try something new and different.

My good friend Reginald is also a man who loves to eat. Now that I think about it, maybe that is why we get along so well. A few years ago, I brought him into my YouTube inner circle of people who do food reviews and he found his voice on the platform rather quickly. It helped that we both have similar tastes in food but we discuss these tastes in two different ways. I still look at food as an adventure in each bite. You need to be able to close your eyes and envision what each flavor is doing to your taste buds. Then you need to see the colors and describe the picture as it becomes clear to you. The flavors coming to life with color tell the story behind that particular meal, and that is what I do. Regg on the other hand, is more a sports fanatic, and so when he takes a bite of a similar burger, he will bring you through the BIG GAME and use analogies that only sports fans can truly appreciate.

When Regg hits the Steakhouse with me, GAME ON! We order up that medium well, and you can almost taste the cut of grass the cow was snacking on. You get that hint of butter, and if by chance they decide to season that steak with a little extra love (though more often than not they do not need to) you will taste paradise. Each chew will need to be slow, so that you can experience a nice cut. When I think about it, we cannot appreciate tough and dried out steak, so that is why ordering it well done is never truly on the menu for either of us.

Now Chris, he is not about the meat game and so when we go out to eat, it is a bit different. Chris is more into fish and vegetables. I call him vegetarian for that has been his lifestyle for a long while now. I respect it because he sticks to it, the same way I stick to my meat game! So, we meet in the middle more often than not. I do my best to make sure we hit a spot that will serve up his vegetarian options without missing a beat in flavor.

I brought him along on my YouTube adventures as well and he reviews all the snacks, cakes, cookies, ice cream (things of that nature)! When time is in our favor, we get together for a collaboration on Lay's new flavors of chips or we will find something his palette can handle (that I can also stomach) and things are great because at the end of the day, it is all about having fun with friends and food.

From time to time, I host what I LIKE TO CALL, "Meat & Eats" which is a play on "Meet & Greet" that many of the YouTube Creators like to do with those that subscribe to our channels. Basically, this is the time where you find a location and broadcast it to your subscribers so they can come out to meet with you and perhaps get an autograph and some pictures. Usually I set up a dinner so they can come out and eat with me.

The reality is, we would not be here without the love and support of the community. Not a single person has to watch our body of work nor do they have to share it, but they do! That is a reason to reach out to the community and just say, "Thank You" for your support. Thank you for choosing my channel.

I started "Meat & Eat" to be a bit more personal for I do not look at my subscribers as "fans" but as what I call them, "Foodie Fam," which is short for family.

For one of my Meat & Eat events everything was set at a restaurant called, "Plan B Burger Bar" located in Milford, Connecticut (they have several locations).

We usually host the Meat & Eat here during Bacon Week and all of those who can make it are invited! I sit among family and we share stories and laughter, almost as if you are attending a family gathering where folks sit around the table and catch up.

This goes on for a few hours but the best feeling is having the opportunity to meet face-to-face those who support my efforts on both YouTube and The Rachael Ray show.

It does not stop here! The same way many go out of their way to support me, in return I most definitely do the same by showcasing many local family owned businesses in the Connecticut area.

My friend Jose Perez owns a food truck called, "The Meat Truck" where you can receive up to a half a pound of meat on your sandwich! This man knows exactly how to feed the people. Now mix that in with some caramelized onions, peppers or even some chicken wings on the side and you are stepping feet first into a meat lovers' paradise. But words and pictures in a book only take you so far. This is something that you would need to experience FACE FIRST on your own.

Eating with friends is an unspoken bond that is hard to destroy. Never lose the moment or forget what great memories are created when you take the time to travel and dine with those close to you. I mean, let us be honest.... who really forgets great food?

I am sure right now many of you can think back to one of your favorite restaurants that you took a friend to, just so they too could experience the flavors and of course the conversations that only you and your friend could truly appreciate.

To link the two makes for an amazing experience. Never lose those moments and always step out to make more of those moments with both old and new friends. Remain open to stepping out and going to a new restaurant to create new memories, and of course seek something on the menu worthy of a decent review from you.

I can't be the ONLY person who automatically reviews food in their mind while they are breaking down the flavors within each bite. We are all food critics in our own right and not a single person should fear speaking up about their thoughts.

Contrary to the shows on TV today, not EVERYTHING is amazing everywhere. I always felt that we lost our way when it comes to speaking the truth about food from various locations, and all because we want everyone to WIN.

Unfortunately that is not the case! Every location does not capture home when it comes to an authentic Italian dish or Southern flare!

Not every Shrimp Po-boy on menus will capture the New Orleans spice when it comes to seasoning, and so we must take these dishes at face value and really dissect them for the good, bad, and the ugly! Much like my new *Restaurant Raider* series on YouTube.

I always look forward to YouTube collaborations that I do with like-minded Creators. I still recall one of my first collaborations with Harley of Epic Meal Time. I was in L.A. filming my TV show, *Best Daym Takeout* back in 2013 for the Travel Channel and it was my first trip to L.A.! I was beyond excited and so I posted on Twitter to my "Foodie Fam" that I would be in the L.A. area. Harley was among those to tweet me back and he asked for me to stop by while I was out there. So I did.

Upon arrival, I was introduced to the rest of the Epic Meal Time members, one of them being Josh Elkin who over the years I would become very good friends with. I was also introduced to Ed Bassmaster who is well known for his prank channel on YouTube (One of the BEST IMO).

Harley set up a collaboration on their channel called, "Luther Lasagna." Just imagine a regular lasagna for a moment and now make it roughly ten times its normal size, flooded with fast food cheeseburgers! When it comes to super-sized meals, Epic Meal Time holds the crown on YouTube, without a doubt.

To cross-promote channels, Harley agreed to also do a food review on my channel, In-N-Out Burger, which was also the FIRST time I had a review of anything from that chain. The energy we delivered in both videos had our subscribers going crazy and they all loved the collaborations between two Food channels. This would spark more collaborations with my channel, but that is the point of growth on YouTube, collaborating with friends and creating the very best content for all to enjoy.

Another great friend to enjoy a good meal with is Josh Elkin, host of *Sugar Showdown* on The Cooking Channel. We have done a multitude of Food Related collaborations on both of our channels and that man can put down some food. When I visit him in L.A. or he comes out my way and we get together in New York, it would seem as if our only objective is to find the best bites these various cities have to offer, and we do our best to never go to the same place twice. It is all about portions, presentation and, of course, flavor.

So now, just imagine two great friends, sitting at a table in a 5-star restaurant or at a hole in the wall spot that we happened to come across. Regardless, we find the time together catching up and exchanging stories over food is what makes the friendship stronger, no matter how many weeks or months have passed since last seeing each other. The reason we go out and gather with our friends in the first place is to enjoy a moment and create some awesome memories along the way, why not do that with those you hold close to your heart? Josh is known for creating exquisite breakfast items and even creating some monstrous dishes too, but his new focus is elevating breakfast and taking it to the next level. Giving a new meaning behind those plain omelets you like so much. There is not much that Josh cannot make happen in the kitchen, for if his back is against the wall and he is given the basic of ingredients, he will come out swinging with something that will truly make your taste buds sing. So that is why we mesh so well. He loves to cook and I love to eat!

Why not find those hidden gems, so that you can write about them later and or share that experience with friends and family? The point of stepping out, is all about change and chasing after something different. Sure, you can do it on your own, but again, food you enjoy with a friend or two is just something that nobody can take from you. And, what is most important, you get to travel abroad to tell your story. The world is watching, so what are you waiting for? GET OUT THERE AND EAT!

CHAPTER 8

EATING ACROSS AMERICA

NOW THAT YOU KNOW why I love to eat at local spots,

food trucks, and those hidden treasures in every city, I think it's time I share some of my favorites (besides those I mentioned in earlier chapters). I can't claim to have eaten at all of these. Some I have, while others I have heard through comments, blogs, friends, and my Foodie Fam that they are can't-miss places. In no way did these eateries contact me. This is just me showing love to those who keep the food first.

THE FOODIE FAM FOOD TRUCKS TO TRY

1. Crepes Bonaparte, CA
2. The Tasty Yolk, CT
3. V-Grits, KT
4. Roti Rolls, S.C.
5. Wok n Roll Food Truck, OH
6. Guerrilla Street Food, MO
7. The Fat Shallot, IL
8. Cow and Curd, PA
9. Dump n Roll, PA
10. HipPops, FL
11. Ox 'N' Bull BBQ, NE
12. Urban Sugar, ME
13. Areyto, CO
14. The Short Leash Hotdogs, AZ
15. Caspian Kabob, OR
16. FukuBurger, NV
17. MOFU, NC
18. Waffle Crush, AZ
19. The MEAT, CT
20. The Cheese Truck, CT

1. CREPES BONAPARTE, CA

Crepes Bonaparte recreates the experience of enjoying French crepes on the streets of Paris, France with made-to-order breakfast, lunch, and dessert-style crepes. Crepes Bonaparte has been featured on Food Network's *The Great Food Truck Race* and Cooking Channel's *Food Truck Revolution* and *Eat Street*.

2. THE TASTY YOLK, CT

The Tasty Yolk was started out by two child hood friends: Eric Felitto and Mike Bertanza, Felitto being a Chef by trade and Bertanza a banker. The two are in a mission to bring the tastiest breakfast treats to Fairfield County Connecticut and possibly the world!

3. V-GRITS, KT

In 2014, looking to broaden her own vegan food business, Louisville's Vegan Temptress, Chef Kristina J. Addington, was the first plant-powered chef to appear on and win Food Network's culinary competition *Cutthroat Kitchen*. She used the prize money, along with a successful crowd sourcing campaign, to start the V-Grits food truck along with partner Jeff Hennis. V-Grits (an acronym for vegan girl raised in the south) has attended or hosted over 125 events in its hometown of Louisville, serving southern-style vegan meals.

4. ROTI ROLLS, S.C.

Roti Rolls has been voted Best Food Truck in Charleston four times in their history. They have been featured on The Cooking Channel, Food Network, Travel Channel, National Geographic, and many others. Recently, Forbes Magazine named them "The 6th Coolest Truck in the Nation." You can find them at Bonnaroo, Shaky Knees, Wannee, and many other festivals. As they continue to bring the funk.

5. WOK N ROLL FOOD TRUCK, OH

Husband and wife team, Matt Bolam and Tricia McCune, have been cooking together for a long time. Tricia was a vegetarian working at KFC after high school, in 1999, when she met Matt and he would purposely drop big globs of mashed potatoes onto her shoes because he thought she was cute. When Tricia's dad got sick with Parkinson's, Matt moved in and took over cooking for the family. They all loved his food as much as he loved making it. Before Tricia's father passed away he told Matt, "f I had the money I would open you a restaurant." That was the start to their dream of opening a food business.

In 2013 Tricia battled and conquered thyroid cancer. After that she knew they couldn't put their dream on hold any longer. Matt was very focused on Asian food. He researched, studied and experimented with Vietnamese and Korean dishes extensively. It is their favorite food and it seemed like a perfect fit to start a business. In 2014, Wok n Roll Food Truck was born with a mission to show people there is Asian food outside of the red and white Chinese takeout menus.

6. GUERRILLA STREET FOOD, MO

Guerrilla Street Food offers a new chapter to the storied food culture of the Philippines. With unassuming food truck beginnings, Guerrilla Street Food now operates two restaurants in St. Louis, serving inventive Filipino and Filipino-inspired food. The casual and affordable concept began with founders Brain Hardesty and Joel Crespo. With Joel's Filipino heritage combined with Brian's culinary pedigree, Guerrilla Street Food ignited an unfound excitement for the Southeast Asian cuisine in St. Louis.

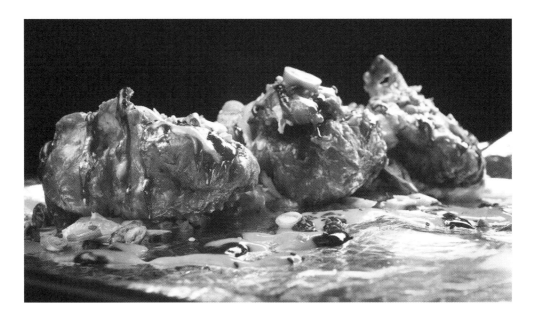

7. THE FAT SHALLOT, IL

The Fat Shallot was started by husband and wife duo Sam Barron and Sarah Weitz. The couple were among the very first to open a cook-on-board food truck in Chicago after the city passed legislation allowing for real food trucks to hit the streets. Sam was a cook and chef for eight years prior to The Fat Shallot cooking in New Orleans, Spain and Chicago. The Fat Shallot strives to serve sandwiches that are memorable, unique and above all the best version of that sandwich that you've tasted. Go find them at one of their two food trucks or at their stationary location in Chicago's Loop.

8. COW AND CURD, PA

It is not a mozzarella stick! This declaration became such a part of The Cow and the Curd's vernacular that the owners had to trademark it. Borrowing the adage of doing one thing and nailing it, this national award-winning food truck has done just that. They have one item, Wisconsin beer battered cheese curds; and boy do they get it right. Taking the country by storm in 2013, The Cow and the Curd sells approximately twenty tons of fresh Wisconsin cheddar curds per season. Neither of the owners, husband and wife, Rob Mitchell and Laura Windham, knew much about the food scene. He was a retired English teacher and she is a psychologist. However, they did know that cheese curds weren't a thing YET on the East coast and they were determined to change that via an amazing product and an exceptionally branded food truck. Fortunately for bars and restaurants, The Cow and the Curd has also added wholesale distribution to their repertoire.

9. DUMP N ROLL, PA

The Premier Dumpling and Roll Specialist. Dump n Roll's concept is to utilize the art of making dumplings and spring/egg rolls as a springboard for our culinary approach. They've raided the world's spice rack as they take inspiration from the entire globe.

By combining quality, value, consistency and the best service possible, they provide an experience to all their guests like no other. They form bonds and relationships that will keep patrons going back long after their first bite. Beyond their passion for food, they believe there's a paradigm shift happening in the global consciousness on many levels. "Impossible actually means I'M POSSIBLE" is their motto.

10. HIPPOPS, FL

HipPOPs founder Anthony Fellows has owned, managed, and operated food service businesses for more than two decades, including experience with frozen desserts dating back to 1990.

Now, he takes hip to a whole new level with HipPOPs.

"This is the hippest way to eat gelato and sorbet. You can hold it in one hand. It's portable, customizable, and not the same-old frozen dessert on a stick." In addition to an impressive resume of experience, Fellows' inspiration for HipPOPs came from his father, who says "If you get up every day and do what you love, it's not work."

11. OX 'N' BULL BBQ, NE

OX 'n' Bull BBQ started in 2001, after a birthday hosted by Mark and Angie for their the four-year-old son. Dozens of family members and friends commented on the style and taste of the food that was served. Mark had his degree in culinary arts, cooking had always been a passion, whereas education and teaching were Angie's.

As time has gone on, their ideas for the business have evolved. They don't compete as much as they used to, however their goals have not changed: they continue to offer fresh, delicious food for reasonable prices, and deliver your order with a smile, a story, and a shared love for good food and fellowship.

12. URBAN SUGAR, ME

Welcome to Urban Sugar Donuts a sweet shop and mobile food truck! They started as a food truck in the Portland, Maine area and are on the move, recently opening their first brick and mortar location at Sugarloaf Mountain. Hot and fresh bite-sized gourmet donuts are their specialty. They like to offer both sweet and the savory varieties, so whether you are seeking a sugar rush or not, we have something for you! Also, check out their always changing selection of baked goods and pastries, and of course, don't forget the coffee! They proudly purchase fresh, locally roasted coffee beans in addition to using as many other locally sourced products from some of the great farms right in the state of Maine.

13. AREYTO, CO

In May of 2016 Erik and Yari open Areyto Food Truck to the public with the objective of bringing something unique and different to the city of Denver as there was a huge need for the presence of Puerto Rican cousine in the city. The menu consists of Mofongo which is the plate of Puerto Rico, plantain sandwiches which are their best sellers, cheeseballs, rice with pigeon peas, steak, chicken and fried pork, empanadillas, tostones, amarillos etc.

Within their first year in business, Areyto won Best Food Truck in the city by the Denver A List. In August of 2017 they were also recognized in America's 100 Best Food Trucks by Gourmandize, featured on MSN. To this day, their mission remains the same: to bring great customer service and quality food each and every time people visit them.

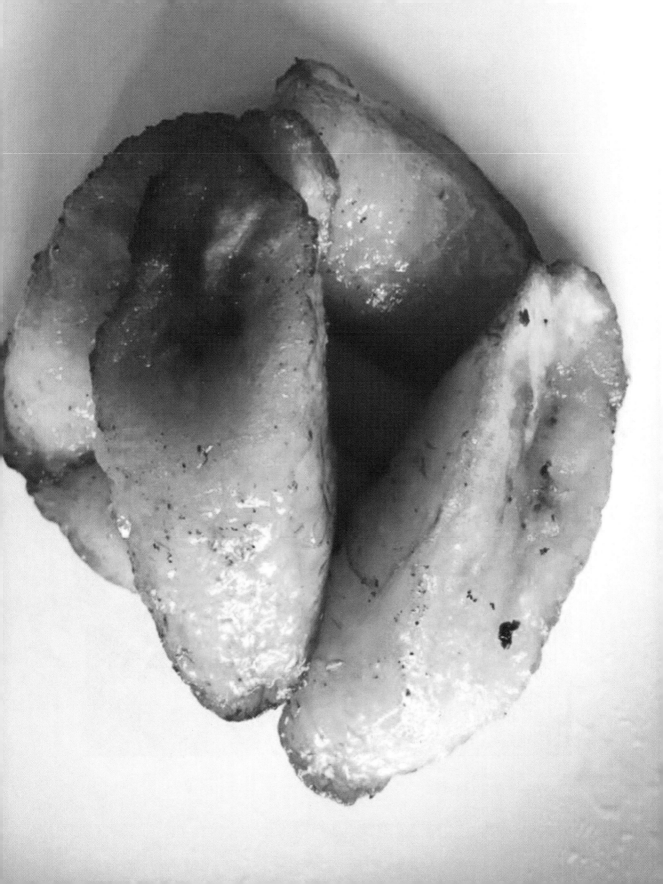

14. THE SHORT LEASH HOTDOGS, AZ

A husband and wife team wanted to try something different, and so they quit their jobs in banking and design and started a gourmet mobile food truck. They started this business because they believe in doing the things you love in life, eating well, and surrounding yourself with people who make you happy. Short Leash Hotdogs and Rollover Doughnuts combines these things and allows them to work with each other.

15. CASPIAN KABOB, OR

When Victor married an American and immigrated to the U.S. in 2000, he missed the rich flavors of the kabobs served on the streets of his hometown in Bandar-Anzali, Iran, located on the Caspian Sea. He began trying to replicate the recipes from his mom's kitchen and his hometown streets.

Over the years, his wife's family in New York looked forward to get-togethers in anticipation of the aromas and flavors of Victor's grilled meats, steamed basmati rice, and freshly chopped salads. In 2013, a move to Portland, Oregon changed his fate. Victor opened Caspian Kabob, Portland's Persian Food Cart. Caspian Kabob's mission is to advance cultural understanding through culinary taste.

16. FUKUBURGER, NV

Vegas first gourmet truck and favorite burger. In the world's service-industry capital FukuBurger was started with a vision of building an off-strip, food-centric community. FukuBurger's mission is simple: deliver excellent food and friendly service at an affordable price to Vegas's own. All-American burgers with a Japanese twist for those who don't take life too seriously.

17. MOFU, NC

Sunny and Sophia started their journey to food by dreaming about building and running a food truck in 2013. With the help of a successful Kickstarter, they finished building the truck and started service in 2014 as a truck that sold dumplings and pho cheekily called the "Dump Pho King Truck." After a year in operation they were approached by Food Network and invited to compete, along with their high school friend Becca Plumlee, in Season 6 of the reality TV show *The Great Food Truck Race* with Tyler Florence under the name "Pho Nomenal Dumpling Truck." Despite setbacks, including a blown engine in the very first episode, the truck eventually went on to become the first and only all-female team to ever win a season of *The Great Food Truck Race*. After being crowned champions of Season 6, Sunny and Sophia decided to keep the "Pho Nomenal Dumpling Truck" name and put their $50,000 winnings from the show towards their brick and mortar restaurant—MOFU Shoppe.

Sunny and Sophia met their Executive Chef, Chef Schaumann, at the beginning of their food journey when both the Dump Pho King Truck and Sol Tacos (Chef Schaumann's previous truck) were just starting out. After a few years of trucking, Chef Schaumann eventually sold Sol Tacos and joined the Pho Nomenal Dumpling Truck's team. The menu, while initially inspired by Sunny and Sophia's love of food, is steered by his innovation and passion.

The final piece of the MOFU family was the addition of Mattew Kenner—owner of Milk Bar and Anchor Bar. His knowledge of the Raleigh area and extensive experience in the hospitality industry are the backbone of MOFU Shoppe's cocktail and beverage offerings.

18. WAFFLE CRUSH, AZ

Waffle Crush was created by two best friends who had a love for Belgian waffles. They created an amazing recipe that can not be topped! They have two trucks that go out to events all over the Phoenix Valley, from public events to private corporate events and weddings. Waffle Crush serves gourmet liege waffles made from dough with infused pearl sugar. The dough is cooked fresh on irons where the pearl sugar melts, creating an amazing caramelized coating on the outside, while leaving it soft on the inside. They have several signature waffles and a wide variety of premium toppings to create your own custom waffle, including the best homemade whipped cream! They also have seasonal waffles that come out for a limited time throughout the year which include Peaches, Pumpkin Cheesecake, Strawberry Cheesecake, Cinnamon Roll and their unforgettable Gingerbread waffle with a special holiday frosting!

19. THE MEAT, CT

The MEAT truck is a butcher shop inspired, gourmet sandwich truck. It's the brainchild of a self-proclaimed MEAT addict. Jose Perez, had long envisioned starting a food truck business centered on his favorite thing to eat, MEAT. Their mission is to build a sandwich truck with an emphasis on quality and freshness. The concept is handcrafted, MEAT inspired sandwiches and dishes with the MEAT, being the main attraction.

20. THE CHEESE TRUCK, CT

Caseus Fromagerie Bistro is located in New Haven, CT. Their mission is to provide New Haven with a fun and comfortable neighborhood fromagerie and bistro presenting simple traditional food with respect for the environment, knowledge of the product, and passion for pleasurable eating....

CHAPTER 9

THE FOODIE FAM SUPER OFFICIAL MAP TO EATING ACROSS AMERICA

TO WRAP UP THIS BOOK, I thought I should map

out the staples of each state so that you all can drive across this country and taste, bite by bite, the BEST DAYMN DISH every state has to offer. There will undoubtedly be some disagreement here. Some states have their one, Super Official dish while others have a few. But since I can only include one (blame my editor) then I imagine this might spark some debate. However, Foodie Fam, remember that friendly debate is always a good thing. These are simply my loves in each state. Who knows, some of you might not even associate the dishes I pick with the state. Feel free to share what you believe to be your home states signature dish on social media with the hashtag: #EatingAcrossAmerica.

Jump in, buckle up and pitch in for the gas money because we're about to go on the taste buds drive of a lifetime!

FLORIDA

We start down south in the Sunshine State: Florida. Off the bat, we have a debate. Cuban cuisine, Seafood, or citrus? If you've been to Florida, then you know what I mean. They take their seafood (whether it be lobster, fish, or alligator) very seriously in Florida. They also have major influences from the Caribbean resulting in some tremendous flavors. When making my decision, I took all of these things into account. What makes Caribbean food and seafood even better? Acid! From oranges to grapefruits, the juice of these citrus fruits elevates nearly any dish. But none better than the world famous Key West Key Lime Pie.

GEORGIA

Up I-95, we cross the border into Georgia where some will argue for BBQ and fried chicken, but those who know the truth know that Georgia is the Peach State. Peaches can be enjoyed in their natural state, as preserves and jams, or if you know what is good for you, as pie. Specifically, Georgia Peach Pie.

ALABAMA

Not used to starting off with desserts? Not to worry, we can find some savory by turning left towards Alabama where the only thing they take more seriously than their football is their Fried Green Tomatoes. Roll Tide!

MISSISSIPPI

Continuing on this culinary road trip you'll want to make sure to indulge a bit. And nothing says indulgence better than Mississippi Mud Pie. It is believed that this delectable and dense chocolate cake overload is typically served with a side of ice cream is named after the banks of the Mississippi River.

LOUISIANA

After such a great blend of salty, crunchy and tangy you need something spicy, right? I bet we can get some great Cajun or Creole spices in Louisiana. But should we go Gumbo or something a little more to-go friendly like a Po' Boy? Maybe back to the sweet with some Beignet? Nope, for me it is all about the Jambalaya.

ARKANSAS

Falling under the category of "don't knock it until you try it," Arkansas' contribution comes in the form of a tasty invasion. The Fried Catfish is a southern staple that makes the best of an invasive species. At times you'll hear this dish described as having a "muddy taste," but for anyone who loves seafood—this is a must try!

OKLAHOMA

Nothing goes better with a good piece of fried fish than just as crispy chips... right? Wrong! That may how they do it over in England, but here in the south, particularly in Oklahoma, the perfect accompaniment to any hearty protein is fried okra. But not just any kind of fried okra, cornmeal crusted deep-fried okra. Giving the crunchy greens a hash brown-like color, this southern staple is great as a side dish or midnight snack.

TEXAS

A slight detour south, and we enter the Long Horn State. Home of the Cowboys, the Alamo and BBQ, it's difficult to know exactly what food to pick from Texas. The Mexican influence is prominent in the cuisine, from fully loaded nachos to spicy interpretations of their BBQs. But nothing is more synonymous with Texas than slow, smoked brisket.

NEW MEXICO

Texas' neighbor to the west, New Mexico, takes its name very seriously. If you thought the Mexican food inspiration was strong in Texas, then you're in for a fantastic flavorful surprise. New Mexico blends what some would argue is *the* American dish (a good ol' cheeseburger) and adds the signature Green Chili Sauce that came to us from south of the border.

ARIZONA

As the Mexican-infusion part of our Foodie Fam road trip continues, we have to make a stop in Arizona and enjoy a deep-fried Chimichanga. What is a Chimichanga, you ask? It's a beautiful accident. The story goes that it was born out of intense heat and fire; not unlike a famous mother of dragons, when the owner of a local restaurant dropped a finished burrito into the fryer. This fried burrito is now the symbol of everything wonderful that can come when you mix the best parts of two wonderful cuisines.

CALIFORNIA

We've made to our first stop against the Pacific…so we have to have some seafood dish, right? Not necessarily. California presents a unique challenge as it has influences from across the globe. From the early settlers, to Japanese immigration, the gold rush influx and of course the Mexican and Central American influence. Rosco's Chicken and Waffles is a spot and dish that comes to my mind instantly. But it doesn't feel uniquely California. However, Fish Tacos do. Crispy, crunchy and always perfectly paired with local avocados, Fish Tacos are the perfect dish to eat by the Pacific.

NEVADA

What can't you eat in Nevada? Sure, Vegas offers up every kind of dish imaginable, but the entire state is really a foodie mecca. For me, the fact that you can go from world-class sushi to perfect medium rare steak speaks volumes to just how talented the cooks in this state are. But let's be honest, if you're driving through the country, a stop in Nevada means a few responsible games in the casino and a few more responsible drinks in between. That's why I think if you are ever in Vegas, your first foodie choice is a good drink to start the night.

UTAH

They say only two things are guarantees in life: death and taxes. I would like to add a third one to the list, hangovers after a night in Vegas. So, as we continue our trip across the Foodie Fam staples, we'll make a stop in the great state of Utah. Why? Because I've heard their Funeral Potatoes are a great way to mend a broken heart, honor a passed loved one, and recover from the sins of Sin City.

COLORADO

Colorado Green Chili is the Rocky Mountain's interpretation of traditional chili. It's a fantastic dish that warms the body and soul. But I would be remiss if I didn't mention the taboo Rocky Mountain Oysters. What are Rocky Mountain Oysters you ask? Well, it is best to think of them as a western delicacy. While technically a Canadian dish, they are a big part of Colorado and mid-western cuisine. So next time you are in Colorado and can only enjoy one meal while watching a Broncos or Rockies game, you'll have a tough choice to make.

KANSAS

As we continue to loop easterly towards my hometown, we approach what many would argue is the BBQ capitol of the world. Kansas City BBQ is a true wonder. The perfect mesh of smoke, liquid, dry and moist. The meats, typically ribs, though they do not discriminate, rubbed with spices, slow-smoked over a mixture of carefully planned woods and enjoyed with a slathering of sauce. This is not a meal to be rushed in your truck during your lunch break. Instead, break out the thick napkins and prepare to enjoy yourself.

MISSOURI

How do you follow up world-class BBQ? With Italian food, of course. Well, sort of Italian. Down I-70, we continue to drive until we arrive in beautiful St. Louis. It is here that we pull up a chair at the local Italian spot for some Fried Ravioli. While many still debate the origins of the dish, one thing is for sure, you won't find a better interpretation of anywhere outside of St. Louis.

TENNESSEE

As the miles keep piling on, so do the calories. But that is a good thing; trust me. Because, after killer sauce ribs and deep-fried ravioli, we now get to enjoy crispy, flavor-packed Dry Rub BBQ. The state of Tennessee cannot be visited without a stop in Memphis for some perfectly seasoned BBQ. They take their dry rub so seriously in this state, that many places will keep the recipe locked up with only a few people knowing every ingredient.

SOUTH CAROLINA

It's been a while since we've seen the Atlantic, but here we are again on the east coast. After a full trek west and back, I know I am dying for some good, southern comfort food. And nothing says east coast food and comfort like Shrimp and Grits.

NORTH CAROLINA

Turning north now, we continue with the pattern of one state BBQ, one state not. North Carolina, aside from being a great inspiration for Petey Pablo, is also the state that gave us the Pulled Pork Sandwich. It is our answer to the only problem with BBQ up to this point, that it does not travel well. The North Carolina Pulled Pork Sandwich is perfect for the road trip as you eat your way through this great nation. Sure, it can be messy, but it wouldn't be BBQ if it wasn't.

VIRGINIA

While we are on the topic of portable food, Virginia and their Ham Biscuits truly are the MVP. This perfectly sized sandwich is as flavorful as it is simple. Sweet and savory country ham on a homemade biscuit. It can be served with eggs or preserves for breakfast or as a hidden midnight snack. Sometimes the best things in life are just that easy.

WEST VIRGINIA

If Virginia invented the simplicity of ham + bread = delicious, then West Virginia perfected it. Now that is not to take away from the country ham, but if you are looking for a variation with a little more heat to it, look no further than the Pepperoni Roll found near the Appalachian Mountains. Not quite a sandwich, pizza or calzone this to-go meal is a little bit of everything.

KENTUCKY

If you are like me, you are enjoying the life out these portable meals. To me, there is nothing like a great to-go sandwich that you can eat as you drive down an empty road with the windows down and your favorite tune blasting. And that's exactly what you should do as you enter Kentucky. But the sandwich we're going to enjoy here is not one we can drive with. This open-faced treat is best enjoyed in a table, as it cannot be rushed. Instead, find the best spot locals are bragging about when it comes to the Kentucky Hot Brown.

ILLINOIS

Oh boy.... I am about to anger some Foodie Fam here. Illinois is the home to some amazing food. The most recognizable of those is undoubtedly the Chicago-Style Deep Dish. But that is not my choice. As you've seen from the lead-up of the past few states, I am a man of many tastes. But you can get to my heart with the right sandwich. And the Chicago Italian Beef is just that sandwich.

IOWA

Crossing over from Illinois into Iowa, we enter the true heart of American farming. And for many here that means enjoying some of the best flavors that the soil of earth produces. Sweet Corn is one of those flavors. Trust me on this one. The corn here only needs but the simplest help of a hot grill to char and some garlic salt to brighten the flavor.

NEBRASKA

As we continue west back to the Pacific, we drive into Nebraska, home of the cornhuskers but not our corn dish. Instead, the meal that you just can't skip is a cross between winter comfort and convenience. The Handheld Meat Pie is exactly that. A dish you enjoy for its warming flavors packed into the perfect pocket.

WYOMING

Wyoming. Chicken. Fried. Steak. That's the result of a southern recipe embraced by northern ingredients. You take the preparation of golden-crisp chicken and apply it to the meats that are generally seen as less. Chuck, round, and at times flank. You coat them, fry them, and enjoy everything Americana that they represent. That's the true definition of iconic and American food.

IDAHO

For a while on our road trip we were eating BBQ, then we moved into sandwiches. And now we've entered into the world of breading and frying. If you liked the Chicken Fried Steak, then you are going to lose your mind when you taste Idaho's Finger Steaks.

OREGON

It's been a while since we've had something sweet. Lucky for us, the next stop is in Oregon, where we'll be able to enjoy the sweet and tart flavors of Marionberry Pie. Marionberry is a blackberry that takes the best parts of Chehalem and Olallie berries and meshes them into a wonderful bite. You then take that bite and stuff it into some delicious crust, bake, and before you know it, you've entered pie heaven.

HAWAII

We're back facing the beautiful ocean breeze of the Pacific. It is now time to find a boat and sail west towards paradise. It is there where we'll find Ahi Poke which is quickly becoming the new Avocado Toast. Healthy, easy to prepare, but complex in its flavors, it is no surprise why this Hawaiian staple has moved through the West Coast and across the country. But if you are ever fortunate enough to visit Hawaii, Foodie Fam, then make sure to partake in this seafood bowl that is as fresh as food gets.

ALASKA

From Hawaii we'll need to head north as we journey as far we possibly can while remaining on U.S. soil. Alaska, as you'd imagine, is home to the best salmon anywhere in the world. And I bet you're thinking that you've had salmon roasted, planked, grilled, fried and even in burgers and bagels. But I am here to tell you that if you've skipped out on Salmon Candy then you cannot skip Alaska. Those who have enjoyed this jerky meets salmon dish know that once you go Candy, you don't go back.

WASHINGTON

Salmon continues to dominate our taste buds as we re-enter the continental U.S. It is here in the state of Washington that they prepare the pink fish on a wooden board known as Cedar Plank Salmon. This method of indirect cooking is called planking. It allows the fish to take in flavor from the wood and smoke, creating a taste that cannot be missed.

MONTANA

As we head east for our final trek across this great country, we enter Montana. Montana is home to Yellowstone National Park and Glacier National Park. Arguably, two of the most iconic lands in the U.S. Within these vast areas, stretching from Idaho to Montana, you'll find the humble huckleberry which, when prepared correctly, transforms into one of my favorite pies, and the can't miss food of Montana: Huckleberry Pie.

NORTH DAKOTA

Lefse Potato Crepes, sometimes called Norwegian Crepes, is one of my favorite dishes that we've encountered. Foodie Fam, welcome to North Dakota where, believe me when I tell you, that there just isn't anything like these bites anywhere else. Typically enjoyed during the winter months, the paper-thin flatbreads are lightly browned, paired with sugar and butter, and rolled. Oh, and you can stuff them with anything your heart desires.

SOUTH DAKOTA

Like its sister state to the north, South Dakota adds to the more peculiar meals on our drive around the U.S. Chislic is hard to explain because it is so simple—you take meat and cube it. Generally, it is the more gamey meat. But any red meat will do. After it is cubed, the meat is deep-fried. Like I mean deep, deep-fried—almost like a flash fry. Medium rare, sprinkle some garlic salt, and enjoy the best kept secret in the heart of America.

MINNESOTA

Lutefisk is this fish dish that is treated with lye and dried and I don't know what else. All I know is that I don't like it. Some people, particularly natives to the state, swear by it. But I am here to tell you that if you are in Minnesota, skip the Lutefisk and go straight for the Hotdish...you won't regret it.

WISCONSIN

You think Wisconsin, you think Bart Starr, Brett Favre, Aaron Rodgers, and cheese heads. Though I would argue that they shouldn't wear cheese heads in Lambeau Field. No, all the Packer faithful should be sporting Bratwurst and Sauerkraut heads. Feel free to *at* me if you love your Wisconsin cheese... because it is hard to argue with. But if you are going to argue, Bratwurst Stewed with Sauerkraut is the way to go.

INDIANA

I know what you are thinking Foodie Fam, what's going on here? It's been a quick minute since we've enjoyed one of those road trip-friendly sandwiches, right? Not to worry as the Hoosier State has us covered. Indiana takes their basketball almost as seriously as they take their Pork Tenderloin Sandwich. It is as iconic as it is flavorful. You know you're in Indiana when the pork is three times the size of the buns trying to contain it.

MICHIGAN

Empanadas are a staple that transcends boarders. Throughout South America and in Europe, variations of these baked pasties can be found. But here in the U.S., the best of pasties lives near the Great Lakes. Michigan Pastys are typically shaped in the style of the letter "D" allowing you to stuff them with mouthwatering carrots and perfectly seasoned protein.

OHIO

We are edging closer to the east coast as we enter Ohio. Buckeye Candy, or as the locals simply call them Buckeyes, are a sweet treat made from a peanut butter fudge that is slightly merged in chocolate giving off the appearance of circle. This art is done intentionally as it is made to resemble the nut of the Ohio buckeye tree.

PENNSYLVANIA

You know we've arrived in the north east when the temperature drops, the hospitality wavers a bit, and you can smell the rib-eye cooking perfectly with a slathering of cheese melting over it. Provolone is my preference, though you can't go wrong with the bright and gooey yellow cheeses over the steak. Sprinkle in some onions and peppers if you fancy, and you have the defining bite from the City of Brotherly Love and the entire state of Pennsylvania.

MARYLAND

If we've learned anything from this road trip across the country is that the best food doesn't require a fancy tablecloth, silverware, and a waiter. No! *Eating Across America* at its finest is all about the experience that the food brings. And there is no experience that better resembles that Americana than Blue Crabs with a generous seasoning of Old Bay, steamed and served over some newspaper. That's love.

DELAWARE

Who here hasn't had a bag of salt and vinegar chips. They're a go-to snack for parents and kids alike. But did you know they originated in Delaware? Well, sort of. The can't-miss-dish here uses everything we love about salty and tangy coming together, and amplifies it with the natural flavors of freshness and frying. The potatoes are soaked in vinegar, left to cool in the fridge overnight and then fried to a perfect brown finish. A finishing touch of salt and sprinkles of vinegar and you've done Delaware right.

NEW JERSEY

Taylor Ham is Jersey's response to Philly's Cheesesteak in their ever-growing sibling rivalry. If you are familiar with Hawaii's Spam, this is the east coast version. You have a pork-based processed meat that is the key player in the all-too-tasty Pork Roll Sandwich. Add some cheese and a couple eggs and you've got Jersey Breakfast.

NEW YORK

Oh man...you know New York is going to produce some debate. Given all we know about New York and the countless cultures that have crafted this unique city, this won't be no stroll through Central Park. You can't go wrong with Chinese food, amazing broths and noodles, or Italian pizza, perfectly toasted thin crusts. Then you have famous, and I mean legit famous hot dogs. Speaking of street food, gyros, and rice bowls? Subway sandwiches a mile long. Man, the list goes on and on. But for me, it always starts and ends with Buffalo Wings. Spicy, crispy, and everything I want from a road trip dish. They go great with a beer, with friends, in the winter, or during a summer ball game. The next debate is the real one, Foodie Fam: ranch or blue cheese, drumettes or flats? #EatingAcrossAmerica

CONNECTICUT

Welcome to my home state Foodie Fam. If you're familiar with my YouTube channel then you know how proud I am to be a part of the Connecticut community. Therefore, it should be no surprise that this was the hardest choice for me in our great American road trip. There are plenty of options from both sweet to savory. Apple Cider Doughnuts, Yankee Fare, Steamed Cheeseburgers (yes, steamed burgers, like that one scene from The Simpsons with Principle Skinner and Superintendent Chalmers), are only some of the options that made this a difficult choice. But at the end of the day, we all know that the Super Official meal from Connecticut has to be New Haven-Style White Clam Pizza.

MASSACHUSETTS

Massachusetts for me is the perfect complement for Connecticut. In my home state, if the fact that we enjoy our clams on pizza seems a bit bizarre to you, then Massachusetts might be a better fit. They go a more *traditional* route with their thick, hearty, and indulgent Clam Chowder. Not to be confused with the Manhattan version, this north-eastern winter staple is creamy, buttery, and a soup that we cannot miss.

RHODE ISLAND

There's not much to write for this next selection. It's not that it does not warrant it, but rather, words cannot do it justice. The only way to really understand this is to fly to Rhode Island in the middle of the summer. Find the hottest day you can, plan a day at the park, maybe a BBQ with friends and family, and when it is all said and done, enjoy a legendary Rhode Island Frozen Lemonade. It'll be a day, and a drink, you'll never forget. Just no spoons!

NEW HAMPSHIRE

New Hampshire's entry as we near the finish line is unique in the sense that it's not named after the state itself. Rather, the dish we have to pull over to enjoy is the New England Boiled Dinner. This is as traditional as you can get. A Daym good serving size of corned beef, a.k.a picnic ham, a little cabbage with potatoes, parsnip, maybe carrot and onions. Really, all the roots are at your disposal.

VERMONT

"As American as Apple Cheese Pie." It doesn't roll of the tongue as well, but man does the sharp cheddar contrast with the sweet apple. I don't think I can sell you on this with words. Truth be told, everyone is hesitant. But Foodie Fam, look in the sideview mirror and reflect. We have put in a lot of miles back and forth this amazing nation so why stop now. Don't be defeated. Instead embrace this Super Official dish from Vermont and enjoy in this new discovery.

MAINE

We made it Foodie Fam. We're here, in Maine. As north east as north east gets in the continental U.S. And what better way to celebrate than with the Maine Lobster Roll. Not just a regional icon, but one of the best dishes the states has to offer. We started with Key Lime Pie and now we put the car in park, get down for the last time, stretch our tired legs, and dive into this simple yet magnificent roll.

CONCLUSION

I will keep this brief. I simply want to thank everyone who has supported me and my dreams over the years. I know that I have been impossible to deal with at times, and often unavailable due to my travels. However, do know that I am always there when I can be. This book has been a passion project and one that I enjoyed writing, with some great memories along the way. I do hope that the readers of this book found it insightful and interesting, for my journey is still one in the making and I can only hope to bring you all along with me in the near future.

LETTER FROM MOM

Daymon S. Patterson...the man, the myth, the legend! His life is an open book. He is straightforward and he sugar coats nothing. I have known him his entire life and he encourages, amazes, and shows others how to attain their life's desires. There is nothing one can't attain if they want it bad enough.

In this book, he takes you on his personal life's journey from beginning, middle ,and present. There is no end because he is ever evolving, ever growing, and ever constant in his endeavors. He reaches, he teaches, and he entertains the masses through his food reviews, his spoken words, his guidance, and unending zest for what matters.

I truly hope all have enjoyed this book and gotten some more insight into the author and what motivates and drives him.

With Love, Mom,
Valerie Patterson